The World's First Hydrogen-Powered Superyachts

From Project 821 to a Sustainable Horizon: Charting the Course of Luxury Marine Transportation

Amanda Joseph

All rights reserved. No part of this publication may be reproduced, distributed, or transmitted in any form or by any means, including photocopying, recording, or other electronic or mechanical methods, without the prior written permission of the publisher, except in the case of brief quotations embodied in critical reviews and certain other noncommercial uses permitted by copyright law. This book is a work of nonfiction. While the author has made every effort to ensure the accuracy of the information contained herein, the author and publisher assume no responsibility for errors or omissions, or for damages resulting from the use of the information contained herein.

Copyright © 2024 by Amanda Joseph

Contents

Introduction
    Brief Overview of the Superyacht Industry

    Introduction to the World's First Hydrogen-Powered Superyacht: Project 821

The Genesis of Project 821
    Background Information on Feadship and its Commitment to Sustainability

    Evolution of the Idea for a Hydrogen-Powered Superyacht

The Technology Behind Project 821
    Explanation of Hydrogen Fuel Cells and their Application in Marine Propulsion

    Challenges and Innovations in Storing and Utilizing Hydrogen Onboard

Design and Features
    Overview of the Exterior and Interior Design by RWD

    Description of Luxurious Amenities and Living Spaces on Board

Environmental Impact and Sustainability

- Discussion of the Environmental Benefits of Hydrogen Fuel
- Potential Impact of Project 821 on the Superyacht Industry's Sustainability Efforts

Challenges and Future Prospects

- Examination of the Challenges Faced During the Development of Project 821
- Speculation on the Future of Hydrogen-Powered Yachts and Advancements in the Industry

Conclusion

- Recap of the Significance of Project 821
- Final Thoughts on the Potential of Hydrogen Fuel Technology

Introduction

The superyacht industry epitomizes luxury, sophistication, and opulence on the high seas. These vessels, typically measuring over 24 meters (79 feet) in length, are synonymous with extravagance and serve as the ultimate status symbol for the world's elite. From sleek exteriors to lavish interiors equipped with state-of-the-art amenities, superyachts represent the pinnacle of maritime engineering and design.

Brief Overview of the Superyacht Industry

The superyacht industry encompasses the design, construction, and operation of luxury recreational vessels tailored to meet the demanding tastes of affluent clientele. These vessels are custom-built to exacting specifications, offering unparalleled comfort, privacy, and indulgence to their owners and guests. With a global fleet numbering in the thousands, superyachts traverse the world's oceans, visiting exotic destinations and providing their occupants with unforgettable experiences.

Superyachts are renowned for their grandeur and scale, often featuring multiple decks, spacious cabins, gourmet kitchens, expansive lounges, and recreational facilities such as swimming pools, helipads, and cinemas. Meticulously crafted by skilled artisans and outfitted with cutting-edge technology, these floating palaces offer a luxurious retreat for discerning individuals seeking the ultimate in leisure and relaxation.

Introduction to the World's First Hydrogen-Powered Superyacht: Project 821

In a groundbreaking development for the superyacht industry, Dutch shipyard Feadship has introduced Project 821, heralded as the world's first hydrogen-powered superyacht. This monumental achievement represents a paradigm shift in maritime propulsion, signaling a departure from conventional fossil fuel-based engines towards cleaner and more sustainable alternatives.

Project 821 stands as a testament to Feadship's commitment to innovation and environmental stewardship. The vessel, measuring an impressive 290 feet in length, embodies the latest advancements in hydrogen fuel cell technology, offering a glimpse into the future of luxury marine transportation. Designed and constructed over a five-year period, this pioneering superyacht represents the culmination of extensive research and development efforts aimed at revolutionizing the industry.

Equipped with hydrogen fuel cells, Project 821 generates power through a chemical reaction that produces electricity without the harmful emissions associated with traditional combustion engines. This revolutionary propulsion system not only reduces the yacht's carbon footprint but also ensures quiet, efficient, and environmentally friendly operation.

As the flagship vessel of a new era in yachting, Project 821 sets a precedent for sustainability and innovation within the superyacht industry. Its introduction marks a significant milestone in the ongoing quest for greener and more eco-conscious maritime solutions, paving the way for future advancements in luxury yacht design and technology.

The Genesis of Project 821

In delving into the genesis of Project 821, one must first understand the visionary thinking and commitment to innovation that underpins its creation. This revolutionary superyacht represents the culmination of years of research, development, and collaboration aimed at pushing the boundaries of maritime engineering and sustainability. From its inception to its realization, Project 821 epitomizes the ethos of Dutch shipyard Feadship and its unwavering dedication to pushing the envelope in luxury yacht design.

Background Information on Feadship and its Commitment to Sustainability

Feadship, short for First Export Association of Dutch Shipbuilders, is a renowned Dutch shipyard that has been at the forefront of luxury yacht construction since its establishment in 1949. With a rich heritage spanning over seven decades, Feadship has earned a reputation for excellence, craftsmanship, and attention to detail. The company's state-of-the-art facilities in the Netherlands are equipped with cutting-edge technology and staffed by skilled artisans who bring each yacht to life with precision and artistry.

Central to Feadship's ethos is a commitment to sustainability and environmental stewardship. Recognizing the imperative to reduce the ecological footprint of its operations, the shipyard has embraced a proactive approach to sustainability, implementing measures to minimize waste, energy consumption, and emissions. From the use of eco-friendly materials to the adoption of energy-efficient technologies, Feadship is dedicated to ensuring that its yachts are not only synonymous with luxury but also with responsible environmental practices.

Evolution of the Idea for a Hydrogen-Powered Superyacht

The concept of a hydrogen-powered superyacht emerged against the backdrop of growing concerns about climate change and environmental degradation. As the maritime industry faced increasing pressure to reduce its carbon footprint, Feadship recognized the need for innovative solutions that would enable luxury yachts to operate in a more sustainable manner. Thus, the idea for Project 821 was born—a bold vision to create the world's first hydrogen-powered superyacht that would revolutionize the industry.

The evolution of this idea was characterized by extensive research, collaboration, and technological innovation. Feadship's team of engineers, naval architects, and sustainability experts worked tirelessly to develop a propulsion system that would harness the power of hydrogen fuel cells to drive the vessel forward. Drawing inspiration from advancements in automotive and aerospace technology, they sought to adapt and refine these concepts for marine applications, overcoming numerous technical challenges along the way.

As the concept took shape, Feadship forged partnerships with leading experts in hydrogen fuel cell technology, regulatory compliance, and safety standards. Collaborating with renowned design firms, such as RWD, the shipyard explored innovative approaches to integrating hydrogen fuel cells into the yacht's design without compromising on performance or aesthetics.

Through meticulous planning, testing, and refinement, the vision for Project 821 began to materialize, setting the stage for a new era of sustainable luxury yachting.

The Technology Behind Project 821

At the heart of Project 821 lies a cutting-edge propulsion system that harnesses the power of hydrogen fuel cells to drive the vessel forward. This innovative technology represents a paradigm shift in marine propulsion, offering a cleaner, more sustainable alternative to traditional diesel engines. In this section, we delve into the intricacies of hydrogen fuel cells and explore the challenges and innovations involved in storing and utilizing hydrogen onboard.

Explanation of Hydrogen Fuel Cells and their Application in Marine Propulsion

Hydrogen fuel cells are electrochemical devices that convert hydrogen gas and oxygen into electricity, with water vapor as the only byproduct. This process, known as electrochemical oxidation, occurs within the fuel cell stack, where hydrogen molecules are split into protons and electrons. The protons migrate through a proton exchange membrane, while the electrons are forced through an external circuit, generating electrical power that can be used to drive motors or charge batteries.

In the context of marine propulsion, hydrogen fuel cells offer several advantages over conventional diesel engines. Firstly, they produce zero emissions, making them an environmentally friendly alternative for powering luxury yachts and other vessels. By eliminating harmful pollutants such as nitrogen oxides and particulate matter, hydrogen fuel cells help mitigate the environmental impact of maritime transportation.

Furthermore, hydrogen fuel cells are highly efficient, converting a greater proportion of the energy contained in hydrogen gas into usable electricity compared to internal combustion engines. This translates into greater range and endurance for hydrogen-powered yachts, enabling them to travel longer distances without the need for frequent refueling.

Challenges and Innovations in Storing and Utilizing Hydrogen Onboard

One of the primary challenges in implementing hydrogen fuel cell technology in marine applications is the storage and handling of hydrogen gas. Unlike conventional liquid fuels such as diesel or gasoline, hydrogen is a lightweight, highly flammable gas that requires specialized storage tanks and handling procedures.

To address this challenge, Feadship engineers developed innovative solutions for storing and utilizing hydrogen onboard Project 821. One key innovation is the use of cryogenic storage tanks, which maintain hydrogen gas at extremely low temperatures (-253°C) to reduce its volume and increase storage density. These tanks are constructed from high-strength materials and equipped with advanced insulation to minimize heat transfer and maintain cryogenic conditions.

Additionally, Feadship incorporated redundant safety systems and protocols to ensure the safe handling and storage of hydrogen onboard Project 821. This includes automated leak detection systems, emergency shutdown procedures, and comprehensive training for crew members on hydrogen safety best practices.

Another innovation is the integration of hydrogen fuel cells with advanced energy management systems, which optimize power distribution and consumption onboard the yacht. By dynamically adjusting the output of fuel cells based on load demand and operating conditions, these systems help maximize efficiency and performance while minimizing energy wastage.

Project 821 represents a landmark achievement in the field of marine engineering, showcasing the transformative potential of hydrogen fuel cell technology in luxury yachting. Through relentless innovation and collaboration, Feadship has overcome numerous challenges to bring this revolutionary concept to life, paving the way for a more sustainable future for the maritime industry.

Design and Features

Project 821 sets a new standard in luxury yacht design, seamlessly blending innovative engineering with exquisite craftsmanship to create a vessel that is as visually stunning as it is technologically advanced. In this section, we explore the meticulous design process behind the exterior and interior of the yacht, as well as the luxurious amenities and living spaces that await passengers on board.

Overview of the Exterior and Interior Design by RWD

Renowned British design studio RWD was tasked with bringing Project 821 to life, both inside and out. The result is a yacht that exudes elegance and sophistication from every angle, with a sleek, modern exterior profile that turns heads wherever it goes.

From its distinctive bow to its sweeping lines and expansive deck spaces, every aspect of Project 821's exterior design has been carefully considered to maximize both aesthetic appeal and functional performance. The yacht's sleek hull is complemented by a striking superstructure, featuring large windows and clean, uncluttered lines that create a sense of openness and connectivity with the surrounding environment.

Inside, RWD has created a world of luxury and refinement, with a design aesthetic that combines contemporary elegance with timeless sophistication. The interior spaces are bathed in natural light, thanks to the generous use of floor-to-ceiling windows and skylights, which provide breathtaking views of the sea and sky.

Description of Luxurious Amenities and Living Spaces on Board

Project 821 is more than just a mode of transportation – it's a floating palace, equipped with an array of luxurious amenities and living spaces designed to indulge and pamper its passengers. From opulent staterooms to state-of-the-art entertainment facilities, every aspect of life on board has been meticulously curated to ensure the utmost comfort and convenience.

The owner's deck is a sanctuary of luxury and privacy, featuring two spacious bedrooms, each with its own ensuite bathroom and dressing room. A private gym provides the perfect space for staying active while at sea, while two offices with fireplaces offer a serene setting for work or relaxation. The living room is the heart of the owner's deck, with panoramic views of the ocean and a cozy seating area perfect for entertaining guests or simply unwinding after a day of exploration.

Throughout the yacht, guests will find a wealth of amenities designed to enhance their onboard experience. A library stocked with books and board games offers a quiet retreat for reading or contemplation, while a private dining room provides an intimate setting for gourmet meals prepared by the yacht's onboard chef.

For outdoor enthusiasts, Project 821 offers ample opportunities for recreation and relaxation. The expansive sundeck features a Jacuzzi and sun loungers, perfect for soaking up the sun and taking in the stunning views. A sea terrace dining room provides an al fresco dining experience like no other, with panoramic views of the ocean and fresh sea breezes.

Project 821 is a masterpiece of design and engineering, offering a level of luxury and sophistication that is unparalleled in the world of yachting. From its sleek exterior lines to its sumptuously appointed interior spaces, every aspect of the yacht has been carefully crafted to provide an unparalleled experience for its passengers. Whether cruising the open seas or docked in a secluded bay, Project 821 is sure to impress even the most discerning of travelers with its combination of style, comfort, and cutting-edge technology.

Environmental Impact and Sustainability

As the world grapples with the urgent need to address climate change and reduce greenhouse gas emissions, the maritime industry has come under increasing scrutiny for its environmental impact. In this section, we delve into the environmental benefits of hydrogen fuel compared to traditional marine fuels, and examine the potential impact of Project 821 on the superyacht industry's sustainability efforts.

Discussion of the Environmental Benefits of Hydrogen Fuel

Hydrogen fuel is often touted as a clean and sustainable alternative to traditional fossil fuels, offering the potential to significantly reduce greenhouse gas emissions and mitigate the effects of climate change. Unlike diesel or gasoline, which produce harmful emissions such as carbon dioxide and nitrogen oxides when burned, hydrogen fuel produces only water vapor and heat when consumed in a fuel cell.

This makes hydrogen fuel an attractive option for environmentally conscious consumers and businesses looking to reduce their carbon footprint and transition to cleaner forms of energy. In the maritime industry, where emissions from shipping contribute significantly to air pollution and global warming, hydrogen fuel could play a crucial role in helping to decarbonize the sector and meet ambitious emissions reduction targets.

By powering Project 821 with hydrogen fuel cells, Feadship is leading the way in demonstrating the viability of this technology for marine propulsion. Not only does hydrogen fuel offer the potential to eliminate harmful emissions from yachts and other vessels, but it also provides a sustainable alternative to finite fossil fuels, which are increasingly expensive and environmentally damaging to extract and refine.

Potential Impact of Project 821 on the Superyacht Industry's Sustainability Efforts

As the world's first hydrogen-powered superyacht, Project 821 has the potential to catalyze a shift towards cleaner and more sustainable practices within the superyacht industry. By showcasing the viability of hydrogen fuel for marine propulsion, Feadship is sending a powerful message to yacht owners, builders, and regulators that sustainable alternatives to traditional fossil fuels are not only possible, but necessary in order to secure the future of the industry.

The environmental impact of Project 821 extends far beyond its own operations, serving as a model for future innovation and investment in sustainable technologies. By demonstrating the feasibility of hydrogen fuel cells for marine propulsion, Feadship is paving the way for other shipbuilders to follow suit and incorporate similar technologies into their own designs.

Furthermore, Project 821 is likely to spur increased demand for hydrogen fuel and related infrastructure, driving further investment and innovation in the development of clean energy solutions for the maritime industry. This could lead to a virtuous cycle of technological advancement and environmental stewardship, ultimately benefiting both the industry and the planet as a whole.

Project 821 represents a significant milestone in the journey towards a more sustainable and environmentally responsible future for the superyacht industry. By harnessing the power of hydrogen fuel cells, Feadship has demonstrated the potential for cleaner and greener marine propulsion, setting a new standard for excellence and innovation in the industry. As other shipbuilders and yacht owners take note of Project 821's success, we can expect to see a growing emphasis on sustainability and environmental stewardship throughout the superyacht industry, driving positive change and lasting impact for generations to come.

Challenges and Future Prospects

In this section, we explore the challenges encountered during the development of Project 821, the world's first hydrogen-powered superyacht. We also speculate on the future prospects of hydrogen-powered yachts and advancements in the industry.

Examination of the Challenges Faced During the Development of Project 821

Developing a hydrogen-powered superyacht presented a unique set of challenges for Feadship and its partners. One of the primary challenges was designing and integrating hydrogen fuel cells into the yacht's propulsion system while ensuring safety, reliability, and efficiency. Hydrogen fuel cells are still a relatively new technology in the maritime industry, and there were few precedents to guide the design and implementation process.

Another challenge was the storage and handling of hydrogen onboard the yacht. Hydrogen is a highly flammable gas, and storing it safely requires specialized equipment and infrastructure. Feadship had to overcome technical challenges related to storing compressed liquid hydrogen at extremely low temperatures (-253°C) and ensuring that the hydrogen remained stable and contained during operation.

Additionally, there were regulatory and certification challenges associated with introducing a new type of propulsion system into the maritime industry. Feadship had to work closely with regulatory bodies and classification societies to develop safety standards and certification processes for hydrogen-powered yachts, ensuring that Project 821 complied with all applicable regulations and requirements.

Despite these challenges, Feadship was able to successfully overcome obstacles and bring Project 821 to fruition, demonstrating the feasibility of hydrogen fuel cells for marine propulsion and paving the way for future innovations in the industry.

Speculation on the Future of Hydrogen-Powered Yachts and Advancements in the Industry

Looking ahead, the future prospects for hydrogen-powered yachts are promising. As the technology matures and becomes more widely adopted, we can expect to see an increase in the number of hydrogen-powered yachts entering the market. These yachts are likely to incorporate advancements in hydrogen fuel cell technology, energy storage systems, and propulsion systems, resulting in improved performance, efficiency, and reliability.

Advancements in hydrogen production, storage, and distribution infrastructure will also play a key role in shaping the future of hydrogen-powered yachts. As hydrogen becomes more readily available and cost-effective, yacht builders and owners will have greater access to this clean and sustainable fuel source, further driving adoption and innovation in the industry.

Moreover, hydrogen-powered yachts are poised to become symbols of luxury and environmental stewardship, appealing to environmentally conscious consumers and setting new standards for sustainability in the maritime industry. As awareness of climate change and environmental issues grows, there is increasing demand for greener and more sustainable alternatives to traditional fossil fuels, making hydrogen-powered yachts an attractive option for yacht owners and charterers alike.

While the development of Project 821 posed significant challenges for Feadship and its partners, it also opened up new possibilities and opportunities for innovation in the superyacht industry. As hydrogen-powered yachts continue to evolve and mature, we can expect to see a brighter and more sustainable future for luxury yachting, driven by advancements in technology, infrastructure, and environmental awareness.

Conclusion

In this final section, we recap the significance of Project 821 as a milestone in sustainable yachting and offer final thoughts on the potential of hydrogen fuel technology in shaping the future of luxury marine transportation.

Recap of the Significance of Project 821

Project 821, the world's first hydrogen-powered superyacht, represents a groundbreaking achievement in the realm of sustainable yachting. Developed by Feadship, this innovative vessel showcases the possibilities of hydrogen fuel technology in reducing carbon emissions and advancing environmental sustainability in the maritime industry.

With its cutting-edge hydrogen fuel cells and state-of-the-art design, Project 821 sets a new standard for luxury yachting while also demonstrating a commitment to environmental stewardship. By harnessing the power of hydrogen, the yacht is able to operate with minimal impact on the environment, producing only water vapor as a byproduct and significantly reducing its carbon footprint compared to traditional fossil fuel-powered yachts.

Beyond its environmental benefits, Project 821 serves as a symbol of innovation and progress in the superyacht industry. Its successful development highlights the potential of hydrogen fuel technology to revolutionize marine transportation and pave the way for a more sustainable future.

Final Thoughts on the Potential of Hydrogen Fuel Technology

As we look to the future, the potential of hydrogen fuel technology in shaping the landscape of luxury marine transportation is immense. Hydrogen fuel cells offer a clean, efficient, and renewable alternative to conventional fossil fuels, making them well-suited for powering luxury yachts and other marine vessels.

With continued advancements in hydrogen production, storage, and distribution infrastructure, hydrogen-powered yachts are poised to become increasingly prevalent in the maritime industry. As awareness of environmental issues grows and regulations on carbon emissions become stricter, there is growing demand for sustainable alternatives like hydrogen fuel technology.

Moreover, hydrogen fuel technology has the potential to drive innovation and economic growth in the marine sector, creating new opportunities for yacht builders, technology developers, and other stakeholders. By investing in hydrogen fuel technology, the industry can not only reduce its environmental impact but also position itself as a leader in sustainable luxury transportation.

Project 821 represents a significant milestone in the journey towards a more sustainable and environmentally friendly future for luxury yachting. By embracing hydrogen fuel technology, the superyacht industry has the opportunity to lead the way in promoting sustainability and innovation on the high seas, setting a new standard for luxury marine transportation in the 21st century.

Printed in Great Britain
by Amazon